THE
CHRISTIAN ANSWER
TO THE
PROBLEM OF
EVIL

J. S. WHALE, D.D.

British Library Cataloguing-in-Publication Data
A catalogue record for this book is available from the
British Library

TO
MOTHER

Contents

Preface to First Edition

THESE Wireless Lectures are here printed almost exactly in the form in which they were delivered during April and May of this year. I have yielded somewhat reluctantly to the request for publication partly because a book on the immemorial problem of evil, however unpretentious, seems even more impertinent than public addresses thereon; and partly because I feel that to print the spoken word is to mix two things essentially different. "It is the mixing of things," said Jane Welsh Carlyle, "which is the Great Bad." My only excuse must be the kind importunity of many of my hearers and correspondents.

To my friend and unofficial teacher, Principal H. Wheeler Robinson, of Oxford, I owe not only the quotations from Wittgenstein (my translation) and Traherne, but also valuable counsel and criticism.

J. S. W.

CHESHUNT COLLEGE LODGE, CAMBRIDGE.
May 1936.

One adequate support
For the calamities of mortal life
Exists, one only, an assured belief
That the procession of our fate, howe'er
Sad or disturbed, is order'd by a Being
Of infinite benevolence and power,
Whose everlasting purposes embrace
All accidents, converting them to good.
WORDSWORTH, The Excursion.

We feel that even if all possible theoretical questions have been answered, our life's problems have not yet been touched. No further question remains, admittedly; and just there lies the answer. We find the solution to life's problem when the problem vanishes. Is not this the reason why man, to whom the meaning of life becomes clear after long doubting, cannot put that meaning into words?
WITTGENSTEIN, Tractatus Logico-Philosophicus, p.186.

But one in a certain place testified, saying, What is man, that thou art mindful of him? or the son of man, that thou visitest him? . . . Thou crownedst him with glory and honour and didst set him over the works of thy hands: Thou hast put all things in subjection under his feet. . . . But now we see not yet all things put under him. But we see Jesus, who was made a little lower than the angels for the suffering of death, crowned with glory and honour.
The Epistle to the Hebrews, ii, 6-9.

I ask them whence their victory came;
They, with united breath,
Ascribe their conquest to the Lamb,
Their triumph to His death.
ISAAC WATTS.

CHAPTER I

Four Classic Answers to the Problem

IF this world is rational what are we to make of the evil rampant within it? So much evil apparently has neither meaning nor purpose. Why do the innocent suffer? If this is God's world and if absolute goodness, wisdom and power are united in Him, how is it that we all desire God's world to be better than it is? How are we to account for its appalling moral and physical evils?

I have undertaken to give four talks on this notorious problem which has vexed thought and tried faith in every age of human history; it will not be surprising therefore if some of you are thinking ''this fellow hasn't half got a nerve''; I am thinking much the same myself. Broadcasting on this age-long enigma may well look like the height of presumption. If the greatest thinkers of the race have wrestled with what St. Paul called ''the mystery of iniquity,'' and what Keats called ''the giant agony of the world,'' what solution can the wayfaring man hope to bring to it? One glimpse into the complexity of the problem will suffice to remind him that any glib talk about the problem of evil will be ludicrously like offering to square the circle or to invent perpetual motion. Strictly speaking, the problem is intellectually insoluble.

Then why bother about it? Why not wash our hands of it? The answer is that evil is a grim fact of experience whether it becomes a problem for the intellect or not. It is no mere academic puzzle for professional philosophers; it presses relentlessly upon us all. Though we cannot solve it, we may not disregard it. No one can make light of disease, slavery, war or famine, least of all the Christian, who cannot but believe in the love and providence of God. Indeed, it is the Christian belief in God which constitutes the problem in all its known acuteness. If the world is the creation of omnipotent goodness, what is the origin and meaning of the cholera germ, the cobra, the earthquake, and all the vast fabric of human folly, selfishness and cruelty which makes evil so terrible and universal a fact of human experience? Faced with the sufferings of the innocent can we affirm that God is love? Will not the words just die in our mouths when we try?

I submit at the very outset of this series of talks that it has always proved vain to look for an adequate solution to this problem along purely intellectual lines. The mystery as such will remain a mystery to the last syllable of recorded time, and mere argument ''about it and about'' will be like the argument of the devils in *Paradise Lost,* who sat on a hill debating the immemorial problems of fate and free will ''and found no end in wandering mazes lost.''

This does not mean that we may ignore the intellectual problem: the first two talks have to try to reconcile belief in God with the fact of evil. It means rather—as I shall argue in the third talk—that the real issues of life can be solved not in terms of any intellectual formula, but only in terms of life's experience; that the only actual solution is the practical one coming out of life itself, and that the Christian's answer to the problem of evil is ultimately contained in what he does with evil, itself the result of what Christ did with evil on the cross. For a Christian, the only real solution is the working solution which proceeds from and shares in that triumph of the incarnate Son of God.

With this proviso, then, we begin with the theoretical problem in all its baffling complexity. It is complex because, like most problems, it contains more than one factor. Indeed, it has been called triangular because all thinking about it starts not from one, but from three fixed points. We have already noticed that the problem is most acute for Christianity, and the reason is that for Christianity these three points stand out with uncompromising clearness. It is the Christian faith which has to state most boldly the three axioms which constitute the problem. The *first* axiom is the absolute sovereignty of God, maker of Heaven and Earth. Christian Theism asserts that the universe is grounded in one and only one Will which creates, sustains and orders all things. The *second* Christian axiom asserts something about the character of God; He is love, in all its goodness and holiness; One who is of purer eyes than to behold iniquity. If He were anything less than this He would not be what we mean by God. The *third* Christian axiom asserts the indubitable reality of evil in God's world. Evil, physical and moral, is a terrible fact—the fact which makes our problem.

Given these three presuppositions, Christian thought dare not slur over any one of them in the interests of neat and easy logic. The difficulties and logical contradictions involved may be tremendous, but we have to hold on to our threefold certainty—that God is the Source and Ground of all that is; that God is holy love;

and that God's universe does contain the stark and mighty fact of evil.

The Christian answer to the problem of evil begins, therefore, by rejecting all those tempting solutions which would simplify the issue by getting rid of the triangle. Christianity rejects three classic types of theory each of which tends to emphasise one of the three presuppositions, to the virtual exclusion of the other two. I invite you to look in turn at these three classic ways of grappling with the problem of evil. The first way can hardly be distinguished from a thorough-going determinism (and by determinism I mean what is popularly called Fate; the notion that everything that happens—all our deeds, thoughts and feelings, all the glittering tumult of history—is fixed or determined beforehand, down to the last detail; thus freedom is an illusion because everything happens of necessity). Very well; the first way starts from the absolute sovereignty of God from Whom and for Whom and unto Whom are all things. Nor does it shrink from the logical consequence of this position: it virtually makes God the responsible author of evil. He alone is the determining cause of all that is: therefore all the sin and woe of this world are necessary elements in His divinely predestined plan. So stated, this is a conception, the excessive logic of which is just appalling. I ought to add, however, that it is as a religious rather than as a philosophical conception that it appears again and again in history whenever men have had an awed and exalted sense of the glory and the majesty of the living God; it is found in the theological systems of India and of Islam; great figures within Christendom like St. Paul, St. Augustine and Calvin only just stop short of it; indeed, it rings out with awful clearness in the majestic language of Geneva. There is more than one passage in the Psalms where this high sense that all is of God finds sublime expression; and in a famous passage in Isaiah, the prophet of the Exile dares to express his religious sense of God's sole causality in words which almost sound like blasphemy in our English version:

> I am the Lord and there is none else. I form the light, and create darkness: I make peace *and create evil:* I the Lord do all these things.[1]

That is the exalted language of poetry rather than of precise prose; to those who would dot its i's and cross its t's, making God responsible for evil, a sufficient answer was given by a Dutchman named Robbert Robbertz in the seventeenth century, when two strict Calvinist ministers tried to corner him at the Synod of Dort, with the problem of the origin of Sin. Robbertz remarked drily, "When the first sin was committed Adam put the blame on the woman, and the woman put the blame on the serpent. The serpent, who was as yet young and callow, made no answer. Now that he has become old and confident he comés to the Synod of Dort and says that God has done it".[2]

That story is really a witty expression of the paradox from which you can never get away when grappling with the great problems of the universe. It states the paradoxical truth that God cannot be made responsible for moral evil, even though the possibility of it and the fact of it must always be included within the divine purpose. If sin were necessitated by God, it could not be sin. We cannot believe in sheer determinism. As someone has

---

[1] Isa. xlv, 7.
[2] Söderblom, *The Nature of Revelation*, p. 67 (Oxford, 1933).

said, sheer determinism is sheer nonsense. A universe created at the fiat of such omnipotence would not be the moral universe which our moral consciousness proclaims it to be. It would make our sense of moral responsibility completely irrational. Indeed the helpless instruments of such omnipotence could not be held responsible for anything, were it good or evil. Morality would cease to have any meaning. Whatever it may be in theory, our human freedom is a fact; and in spite of the paradox, irresolvable by logic, that God is the sovereign cause of all that is, and that man is free, we may not define either truth in such a way as to reduce it to absurdity.

So much for one classic type of thought about evil, with its ruthless emphasis on divine predestination. As an answer to the riddle it creates more difficulties than it solves.

We come in the second place to another classic way of thinking about evil, which tends to be preoccupied not with God's sovereign will but with His divine perfection. Taking its stand on the perfect goodness of God, it argues that in reality there cannot be anything wrong with His universe; there cannot be anything intrinsically bad in this world since God is good. That being so, you have to do one of two things with evil.

(i) You can argue, as distinguished systems of thought have done, that the sin and suffering of the world are an illusion, due to our necessarily limited and short-sighted point of view as finite beings, our inability to see things as they really are from the standpoint of eternity. Evil is a delusion of the mind; it is due to what the great thinker Spinoza called "darkness in us." The weariness, the fever and the fret of man's life, the truculent brutalities and degradations of history—all this is the unreal assuming the semblance of the real; it has no existence for the Infinite Being who sees this world of time and sense in terms of eternity. The ultimate basis of this theory in its many forms is pantheism, which identifies God with the universe; God is the whole of things, or the whole of things is God.

Objections to this are obvious but two must suffice here. The first is that we do not get rid of grim facts—greed, lust, bereavement, cancer, insanity—by regarding them as unreal. Though there is truth in the popular theory that pain is due to our minds—since apart from mind it would not exist—the well-known limerick about the faith-healer of Deal is a commonsense exposure of its fallacy.

"There was a faith-healer of Deal
Who said 'Although pain isn't real,
When I sit on a pin,
And it punctures my skin,
I dislike what I fancy I feel.' "

If suffering is all imaginary, why do we dislike it? The hard facts of pain and sin may not be disposed of so easily.

The other objection is that if one of the fundamental elements of human experience is an illusion, this fact is itself an evil; the problem is not solved, it is merely pushed one stage further back. "Darkness in us" would still be a problem clamouring for solution. To say that all suffering is a delusion of man's mind would be to make the existence of that mind the worst of evils; there is not much to choose between pain that is objectively real and mind which necessarily imagines the pain that tortures it.

(ii) So much for one of the two ways of explaining evil if the whole of things is good. The other way— which is, perhaps, only a variant of the first—is to explain evil as necessary to the good of the whole. Evil is not an unfortunate blot which the finished picture can't help having; the blot is essential to its beauty; the artist deliberately put it there; it is an element contributing to the perfection of the whole, like a black cloud in one of Constable's pictures, or like those momentary discords in a symphony which enhance the total harmony. Presumably then, tuberculosis or slums or murder, though relatively bad, are—from an absolute standpoint —good. In the eternal order of things pain and sin are nothing to worry about; they are as necessary to its perfection as are beauty and joy and virtue. Indeed, they are the artistically effective dark background against which all that is good shines in vivid splendour. Like the dark places in Rembrandt's pictures, they make the high lights possible.

But there are several common-sense objections to this dangerous doctrine. The optimism which belittles evil is an immoral optimism. It leaves unexplained vital elements in our moral consciousness; the fact, for example, that our moral distinctions between good and evil are absolute. Wrong is wrong, if the testimony of literature, history and the human conscience is anything to go by. There are certain evil things which a man would rather die than do. The sense of moral obligation is a sacred and compelling thing in man; he cannot doubt that his torturing sense of guilt and estrangement from God when he fails to discharge that obligation is as real as anything in this universe. If you explain away moral evil you explain away that human reaction to it which makes man

man, and differentiates him from an animal or a potato
or a stone.

Again, this doctrine implies that God not only permits
evil (which is obviously true), but that He deliberately
creates it; he purposely does evil that good may come; to
which we need only reply with St. Paul "God forbid!"
The argument that the end justifies the means is as
morally unjustifiable for God as for men.

Again, if the existence of evil is necessary to the good
of the whole, will it not be a mistake to try to get rid of
evil? To lessen evil, on such a hypothesis, will surely be to
lessen the good of the whole; presumably the universe
would be less perfect if its evil were removed; and
therefore suffering men whose sin is ever before them
need not strive to change anything; all their high moral
aspirations, all their dreams of betterment, are vain;
which is absurd. The truth of which this is a distortion is
that nothing in God's world is absolutely and irrevocably
evil; if anything were so, this world could not be the
best of all possible worlds, and the Christian idea of God
would have received a fatal wound. In the second talk I
want to argue that the *possibility* of evil is necessary to
the ultimate good, and that even the fact of evil can
never lie outside the all-embracing and redeeming purposes of God. But that is not to say that evil is really
good, or that the existence of Evil is necessary to God.
All blurring of the eternal distinction between good and
evil provokes the ancient question, "Shall not the judge
of all the earth do right?"

So much for a second classic answer to our problem.
It can solve the difficulty only by denying its fearful
reality.

Now for a third classic way of grappling with the

problem of evil. Can we put it down to the Devil? That is, can we escape from the dilemmas in which determinism or pantheism would involve us, by declaring boldly for dualism? May there not be a creative will other than and opposed to the will of God? This dualistic type of thought takes its dogged stand at the third point of our triangle. It concentrates on the brute fact of evil and virtually denies God's sovereignty. God is not really master in His own house; He is powerful but not all-powerful; He is hindered, limited, by a positive principle of evil which—in the thorough-going forms of this theory—is almost another God. God can only wage war against the Prince of Evil and do His best. A hierarchy of demonic powers is ceaselessly opposed to Him, working woe instead of weal. The language of religion about the powers of darkness means that there is war in the universe; the eternal purpose of God is being crossed by the exactly opposite purpose of ''the Spirit which always denies''; so far from building the city of God it ever seeks to destroy it, and the vast kingdom of evil which we know is the measure of Satan's success.

Crude statements of this theory can be neglected. If we believe in God at all, we believe in One God. His dominion cannot be disputed by another without His ceasing to be what the religious man means by God. Nevertheless, something very like this dualistic explanation of evil has played an impressive role in religious history. Distinguished modern thinkers are not wanting who believe in the Satan of Christian theology. And it is difficult to see how anyone can deny that Jesus Christ Himself accepted a dualism of some kind as a fact of religious experience. Jesus never worked out any formal theory about evil in God's universe; for Him evil was not a conundrum for the intellect but a task for the will. He accepted the fact of evil and dealt with it. He said "An enemy hath done this"; "Deliver us from Evil"; "Now is the judgment of this world; now shall the prince of this world be cast out"; "Every plant which my Heavenly Father planted not shall be rooted up." There, Jesus is speaking the language not of philosophy but of religion. Even though there is a Prince of this World, this world belongs to God the Father. Even though He prays that God will keep the disciples from the Evil One, He is never in any doubt as to the result. Jesus believes in the powers, but He defeats them.

But, even so, this language of religion cannot serve as a philosophical explanation of the mixed nature of the world. Even if there be devils and a prince of devils, the problem as to their origin and existence in God's universe remains. *Why* is the Devil evil? Unless we abandon the specifically Christian view of God, the dualistic explanation merely pushes the problem one stage further back. The problem of evil becomes the problem of Satan or Beelzebub or Mephistopheles; it is no nearer solution for being cast in this more vivid and dramatic form.

So much for a third classic way of dealing with the problem of evil, the way of thorough-going dualism. The Christian finds it no more satisfactory than the other two ways; for, like them, it would solve the puzzle by turning it into something different. As we have seen all along, the problem ceases to be the Christian's problem when it ceases to be triangular, in the sense already indicated.

It is at this point perhaps, that someone will make the

pertinent objection, ''But why cause yourself needless perplexity by assuming that God exists at all? Why not say, as Laplace said to Napoleon, 'Sire, I have no need of that hypothesis'? The problem of evil, which is obviously very acute for theism, does not arise for agnosticism or atheism, and it need not arise for you. Give up this pathetic belief in God, which is causing all the trouble, and there is no longer any problem. Evil will still be an inescapable reality, of course, but there will be no mystery about it. Evil will be what it has always been, just a fact, like the weather, or the Rock of Gibraltar, or Death.   And that's all there is to it!''

To this I would reply that even though the problem of evil vanishes if there is no God, such a hypothesis lands you at once with a new problem, even more intractable than the old, namely the problem of good.

It is certainly true that there is no mystery about evil if there is no creative mind directing the whole evolutionary process. Indeed, if man's mind with its faculty of knowing and valuing and judging, had appeared within a mindless and meaningless universe, evil would have been its natural and inevitable accompaniment. Nothing but acute human suffering could have resulted from such a misfit—from the emergence of feeling and thought amid an order of things alien to both. Man would have become increasingly sensitive to the stern antagonism between himself and his environment; with developing human consciousness, human misery would have inevitably been intensified.

But does our human experience fit such a theory? If this naturalistic account of evolution were true, the fact of suffering would be explained but not the equally real fact of happiness. The sense that life is good at once becomes a problem. Not pain but joy, not evil but good is now the fundamentally irrational thing. If there were no creative mind with which man's emerging mind could find kinship, man's sense of evil would be explicable, but not his sense of good.

Further, if ultimate reality consists of purposeless and directionless happenings how are we to account, not only for man's sense of good but also for his reverence for it—his integrity, his disinterested devotion to a great cause, his heroism, self-sacrifice, love? Whence comes the moral sense, which has such an imperious and compelling way with us? How are we to account for our sense of the sacred which is dearer than life itself? Our inevitable judgment that wrong-doing is always more than mere accident or mistake is a religious judgment, based on our awareness of a spiritual order, a divine order. The problem of evil is what it is just because God has made man what man is, a moral and spiritual being who has his very origin and existence in the creative Word of God. To talk about morality in a non-moral universe is vain.

If someone replies, "Well, but to talk of evil in a moral universe is also vain," I can only invite him to consider in the second talk of this series the justification by Christian theism of the occurrence of evil in God's world.

CHAPTER II

The Answer of Theism

"God's in His heaven,
All's right with the world."

———

BUT how can Browning make Pippa sing like that, when so much is plainly wrong with the world and when Pippa herself is a little ragged girl working the whole year round in an Italian silk mill, "to earn just bread and milk"? It sounds such incorrigible optimism, even though she has a day off and the sky is blue. Is there any justification for it?

If a Christian answers "Yes," how will he account for and justify the occurrence of terrible evils in God's world? It is with this aspect of the notorious problem of evil that I have to deal here.

The evils which men suffer fall roughly into two classes. There are moral evils for which on the whole we are responsible, and physical evils for which on the whole we are not. Slums, bombing, and slavery belong, plainly enough, to the first class; they are foul iniquities and they are our own most grievous fault. Earthquake and typhoon belong to the second class; they involve man in disasters which he can neither cause, control, nor easily avoid. Thus, moral evils constitute the whole problem of sin; physical evils present the problem of suffering, and that in its acutest form, the "undeserved" suffering of the innocent.

This distinction between moral and physical evil is not absolute, of course; there are notorious evils such as famine, disease and grinding poverty which often enough belong to both classes. Though man is not responsible for the cholera germ he is often responsible for cholera; but for his selfishness and inhumanity, his vices and stupidities, cholera could be very largely eliminated. In one sense an outbreak of plague which kills a thousand people in a week is as much a physical evil as the tornado which annihilates a township in half a minute; both are disasters which come out of the blue, as it were. But in another sense plague is a moral evil such as a tornado can never be; human folly, selfishness and dirt have so much to do with causing it that we cannot use the lawyer's language about an "act of God" to explain it. The fact is that physical evil and moral evil, though distinct from one another in principle, are closely bound up with one another in fact.

It is just here, however, that we have to guard against a dangerous fallacy. We cannot believe that there is any inevitable and exact connection between suffering and sin, between a man's misfortune and his character. What we may call the theology of the counting house, with its neat little calculus of rewards and penalties and its bland assumption that a suffering man must be a sinful man, was discredited once and for all by the book of Job. Job's voice is the voice of Everyman, appealing to experience against this all-too-easy formula. The view that God antecedently wills the lightning stroke, shipwreck, cancer, cannot save itself, especially in a scientific age. It is a matter of common observation that

"Streams will not curb their pride
The just man not to entomb;
Nor lightnings go aside
To give his virtues room:
Nor is that wind less rough that blows a good man's
barge."

The simple hypothesis that there is an exact equivalence between merit and award in human life breaks down before the fact of injustice, the fortuitous severity and unequal distribution of suffering. Is it not notorious that a suffering man is not necessarily and not always reaping where he has sown: that those who flourish may have done wickedly? You cannot argue back from sorrow to sin or from prosperity to piety. The doctrinaire contention that there is a precise causal connection between character and fortune is shattered by an appeal to life.

But though this is a dangerous fallacy, we have to add at once that human selfishness and sin, *collectively considered*, will explain much if not most of human woe. We can and must argue back from much human suffering in general to human sin as its cause. If we could eliminate from the problem of evil man's inhumanity to man— itself the outcome of his greed, fear and ignorance, and of the fact that sinful lives interlock to form a vast and organised system of evil—would not the problem have dwindled to relatively trifling proportions? Who will deny that the economic, political and social redemption of humanity would be an easy business if all men suddenly become wise, good, just and loving? Practically considered, therefore, the problem of evil is "the mystery of iniquity": it is the fearful fact of sin—

universal in its range and tyranny—which is the one completely irrational fact in this universe. Ultimately we cannot explain it, whether we appeal to what has been called the Fall of Man, or to Original Sin or to the Devil. These are, at best, great mythological theories which cannot really account for the paradoxical fact, that it is God's world in which evil, physical and moral, occurs.

All that we can do is to begin by recognising that God's world is an evolutionary process working out the cosmic purpose and destined to achieve certain great ends, which include moral ends. Much of this cosmic purpose is necessarily incomprehensible to the finite intelligence of man; but it may have ultimate meanings, which lie and must lie beyond his reach. We cannot hope completely to understand the end of creation; but we know something at least of what it must certainly include. We read at least a fragment of its history which stretches back over two hundred million years into the immemorial past; we have the record of the rocks. And the most significant thing recorded about this vast process is the slow evolution of mind. The process has produced minds able to know the process and to value it, to think and to judge. Not only life but consciousness, not only consciousness but self-consciousness, have come successively into being. The creative mind which directs the whole process, and without which the emergence of man's ideas and values would be unintelligible, is—we believe—ever working to some great End or Ends, and whatever the divine purpose may be in all its infinite significance, it certainly includes that moral order which we call the Kingdom of God.

The bearing of all this on the problem of evil is plain.

Since this is an evolutionary world, it is certainly not the best possible world if by "best possible" is meant "most pleasant," or "most comfortable." Its *raison d'être* is moral progress rather than unalloyed happiness. The universe as moral aims at the highest good, and though this includes happiness it is not to be equated with it. The Christian is no kill-joy, but it is an immediate deliverance of his moral consciousness that this grand theatre of a universe where you and I are players for an hour, is a theatre of moral effort, and therefore that the pleasure-pain principle cannot be the true principle of its interpretation. A world without obstacles, effort and pain would not and could not be a moral order; that is, it would not be a "best possible" world.

Throughout the whole long process, necessity has ever been the mother of invention. All life, including that of man, grows "expert by experiment." An evolutionary world and a "perfect" world are incompatibles; we cannot have it both ways. From the palæozoic era until now we can discern a progressive principle in nature, making the world no safe place for sluggards. Whether you call it natural selection or use the language of scripture about the divine election, it was this principle which drove out the invertebrates, and with the first fishes put backbone—literally and metaphorically—into the story of life. Driving necessity in the shape of arid desert slowly forced the earliest lung-fishes to climb out on to land, and to become the ancestors of the land vertebrates—a tremendous venture which may have taken millions of years and countless millions of organisms for its consummation. Out of adversity qualities were born that made the success of backbone certain, on land and in the sky; out of hardship came our little sisters the birds. Why did the Dinosaurs ultimately perish from this earth which they possessed and ruled for over fifty million years? Probably because in this vast process which refuses to define progress in terms of stagnant ease, the divine election passed them by. Death came from within, not from without.

To ask why this is so—why this is a moral order to be vindicated by free beings and not a paradise of effortless perfection—is ultimately an insoluble question. The world *is* evolutionary and in that ultimate fact the problem of evil is rooted deep. The evolutionary process, like the fact of creation, is part of the ultimate nature of things behind which it is meaningless to try to go. All thinking must begin with what is, and with God as the ground of it. Why God is what He is, is obviously a futile question. To quote Robert Bridges in *The Testament of Beauty:*

"Wisdom will repudiate thee, if thou think to enquire *why* things are as they are or whence they came; thy task is first to learn *what* is . . ."

Very well; on this basis we have now to ask and try to answer two main questions.

The first is this: Granted that physical evils are part of what is, part of the structure of this "vale of soul-making," as Keats called the world; granted that they are the inevitable condition of our growth as free moral persons, necessary accompaniments of what does make for the highest good—is it credible that they are all necessary? Suffering and pain are man's discipline; yes. But are not some, at least, of man's sufferings superfluous, in that the same high ends could be achieved without them? It is the ghastly superfluity of so many of the ills the flesh is heir to, which provokes this question. What can we answer?

It needs little reflection to see that *order* is the *sine qua non* of a moral world; it is the only basis on which moral achievement can be built. If our environment were a chaos rather than a relatively settled order, and if we never knew within reasonable limits what was going to happen next; if water might suddenly freeze in mid-summer; if the specific gravity of lead might at any time become that of thistledown; if pigs might fly or the Houses of Parliament turn into green cheese—man's life would be a nightmare, not merely because it would be unpleasant but because it could have no moral meaning. No vindication of the moral order would be possible in terms of such chaotic indeterminancy. Freedom, in the sense in which religion asserts it, is not indeterminancy; it cannot even exist save in what Butler called "a relatively settled order." The vindication of the moral order by God's freemen can happen only in a universe whose laws are comparatively reliable. Without the fact of gravitation, for example—a fact which can be so dangerous and hurtful to man—man could not build a house nor fell a tree. Again, if fire is to have all the properties which make it so important and precious in man's life, it cannot *not* have the noxious quality of burning a baby trapped in a blazing barn. Necessary "laws" like these are necessarily inexorable; there cannot be assigned to any substance like fire, iron or water now one arbitrarily selected group of qualities, and now another.[1] A world that is to be a suitable stage for man's moral life has to be reliable and regular in its working, and therefore the occurrence of accidents and catastrophes in the causal

---

[1] See F. R. Tennant: *The Elements of Pain and Conflict in Human Life, Considered from a Christian Point of View*, p. 104 (Cambridge University Press).

network of events is no ground for asserting that physical evil, taken as a whole, is superfluous. For the universe is one, throughout; "thou can'st not pluck a flower without troubling of a star"; if there be purpose anywhere it must extend everywhere, and even include what man cannot help regarding as catastrophes and disasters.

Further, to those who endeavour to look at man's life against the background not only of world history but also of eternity—since they cannot believe that death is the end—even fearful natural catastrophes are seen to have had an ultimately beneficent meaning, forcing men to embark on new and hazardous enterprises, and bringing out of pain and tears qualities and achievements of the human spirit which could not, apparently, have emerged otherwise. Look at the perfect build and balance of fishing-boats in which brave men go to sea far up in the North; not for nothing has that functional perfection been secured; there is human life in every line. The people who sit at ease in the floating palace of a luxury liner like the *Queen Mary* are debtors—whether they know it or not—to the immemorial tradition of a seafaring race, to sailors, craftsmen, brave and lonely heroes innumerable who have hazarded and given life through uncounted generations. A study of history like that by Toynbee makes it clear that a challenging environment and man's gallant response thereto have played the decisive role in the birth of civilisations; civilisations are not apt to be generated and cradled in environments which offer unusually easy or soft conditions of life. The Greek proverb stands: "The best things are difficult"; or, as in a more familiar tag: "No pains, no gains."

I hasten to add here that it is notoriously easy to preach smooth platitudes about the discipline of pain;

they just nauseate us because they sound so cruelly complacent; we feel that we have no right to do anything in the presence of suffering but keep a reverent silence. We can all think of brave people who have been beaten down by blow after blow; they suffer in body and mind; they lose their loved ones; the circumstances of their life seem pitilessly hard; to dare to speak words of comfort to them, or even to intrude upon their sorrow at all, seems almost like blasphemy. For things evil are really evil, and even though they contribute to the existence of a greater good than is conceivable without them, they remain a grim riddle which no neat formula will solve. Nevertheless, the point which I am venturing to make here is the one which the sufferers themselves teach us; every hospital ward is eloquent of it; it is an abiding truth which only the sentimentalist will complacently affirm but which only the cynic will bring himself to deny—that suffering, however cruel and undeserved, can and does ennoble men; it is often the occasion and the raw material of the greatest achievements of the human spirit.

> "There is some soul of goodness in things evil,
> Would men observingly distil it out."

That is true, though it is a truth which we can distort with disastrous ease. Shakespeare meant that since the possibility of evil is necessary to the good of the world, taken as a whole, man's divinest endowment lies in the possibility of his triumph over evil, of his transformation of defeat into victory. A Christian has good reason for knowing how true that is as he stands in awe and gratitude before the Cross of Christ and enters into the fellowship of His sufferings. At this stage of the argument, however, I am urging the truth of experience that a world with suffering and bravery in it is better—that is, of greater ultimate worth—than a world with neither in it. Joseph in the ancient story had solved the problem of evil when he said, "Ye thought evil against me, but God meant it unto good."

Here someone may observe: "Yes, the problem of evil presses on us least where we know it best from within and can make moral sense of it. But what of the pain of the animal world, red in tooth and claw, which has been described as one vast conjugation of the verb 'to eat'? Surely the problem of physical evil presses most severely here, simply because animals would seem to have little or no consciousness of alternative ends, or of a moral and spiritual order. How can the moral order make of animal suffering a means to its own vindication?"

This is a very great difficulty, and I will not run away from it by urging that there is in nature much "mutual aid," to quote Prince Kropotkin's phrase. The stark truth which baffles us here is that Nature *is* red in tooth and claw. I can only say that the people who can speak with most authority about animals tell us that though we know little about animal psychology, it is certainly fallacious to attribute to animals our human sensibilities. I am not thinking of the animals which we have domesticated, but of the jungle, the prairie and the ocean; and I learn from those who spend their lives in the study of nature that, according to all the available evidence, animal life is, on balance, happy.

But the vital and humbling point here is surely this: there is continuity in the evolutionary process from the lowest brute creation up to man. What if the development of the sensitive nerves of the lowest animals be a necessary preliminary stage to the creation of a Beethoven or a Leonardo da Vinci? What if we, without them, could not be made perfect? As a modern poet has put it, "This is no argument for indifference to the sufferings of that innocent underworld. It is rather a plea for something like reverence as we confront it." He means that if the conditions which involve animal suffering are those which at our human level are needed to call out man's finest spiritual achievements; if our beneficent human pain is therefore an implicit justification of the pain of amphibian, reptile, bird or mammal, no man with any insight will be smug or complacent at this groaning and travail of the *whole* creation; if he realises that here is one of the conditions of the revelation of the sons of God, he will be more likely to be subdued to contrition and to cry: "God be merciful to me a sinner!"

So much for the first question about physical evil and its alleged superfluity. The other question is concerned with moral evil. Granted that because this is a moral order, freedom is both man's glory and his burden; granted that the possibility of moral evil (cruelty to children, for instance) is logically inevitable if the achievement of the highest good is to be an actuality—is such an achievement worth the terrible cost? This question forces itself upon all thinking people and will not let them alone. Could not God secure the same end without these means? If not, is human life worth while on such conditions?

Well, the fact that few of the world's millions commit suicide is one significant comment on this pessimism. One answer to the indigestion of life so characteristic of Thomas Hardy's novels and poems, is that it is not truly typical of most human experience. The problem of evil is real and intractable enough, but we need not go out of our way to magnify it, nor to deny that there is joy and beauty in life. Thomas Hardy's pessimism has to reckon with a passage like this from Jeremy Taylor:

> "I sleep, I drink and eat, I read and meditate, I walk in my neighbour's pleasant fields and see all the varieties of natural beauty . . . and he who hath so many forms of joy must needs be very much in love with sorrows and peevishness, who loseth all these pleasures and chooseth to sit upon his little handful of thorns."

That is common sense and it will at least prevent our getting the grim problem of evil out of its true perspective. Being morbid about the problem will not help us.

But there is another answer to this wistful question, "Is human life worth-while? Is the moral order worth the terrible cost?" It is that on any other conditions man would not be man. Huxley once wrote that if a higher power would undertake to make him always do what was right, on condition of being turned into a sort of clock, he would close with the offer, since the only freedom he valued was freedom to do the right: freedom to do wrong he would gladly get rid of.[1] It sounds plausible; but the "freedom" of a clock, so far from being freedom, is sheer mechanical necessity. Huxley's hypothesis nullifies his conclusion, because it sells the birthright of human personality; a being incapable of wrong is also incapable of right; he is not a human being at all but an automatic machine. He is not a free spirit

[1] *Collected Essays*, I. 192, as cited by F. R. Tennant in *The Concept of Sin*, p. 158 (Cambridge University Press).

able to learn obedience from the things that he suffers, but a Robot like the traffic-light at the street corner. This, surely, is the meaning of Lessing's profound remark: "If God held in His right hand all truth, and in His left only the ever-active impulse to search for truth, even with the condition that I must always make mistakes, and said to me, 'Choose!' I should humbly bow before His left hand and say, 'Father, give me this. Pure truth belongs to Thee alone.' "

That is, freedom—though it involves grievous error and pain—is the very condition of our being human. There can be no other way for men and women called of God to vindicate the moral order. We cannot have it both ways. It is only in a world where the horrors of war, slavery and prostitution *can* happen, that the learning of self-sacrifice, fellowship and chivalry *will* happen. Indeed, if God were to suppress the possibility of moral evil He would be *doing* evil, for He would be preferring the worse to the better.

There, then, are two of the severest difficulties which belief in God has to face; the fact of physical evil, or suffering; and the fact of moral evil, or sin. Even if the answers of philosophical theology are satisfactory as far as they go, do they go very far? I have been giving answers which I believe to be true and vital; and yet, how unsatisfactory they are—how academic and remote—if left just like that. As I reminded you at the outset, it is our religious sense, our certainty of God, which makes this problem of evil so real. The keenness of our scandal at innocent anguish comes not because there is no God of Comfort, but because there is. We have seen His splendour shining in the face of Christ upon the Tree; and we know. So then, if it be religion which emphasises the problem, it will be religion which alone can give the solution. What does Christianity say to us just here?

The third talk will appeal to faith and life rather than to theory. It will point to history and to God's self-disclosure there in positive revelation. I believe that what has been called "the hunger of natural theology" is satisfied only in the Cross and the Resurrection of the Incarnate Son of God.

CHAPTER III

The Christian Answer

THE Problem of Evil is like the riddle of the Sphinx. The Sphinx was a terrible monster with the head of a woman and the body of a lion, which stationed itself beside the highway outside the ancient city of Thebes. It propounded a riddle to all who passed by, and devoured them because they could not solve it: "What is it that goes on four feet in the morning, on two at noon, and on three in the evening?" Oedipus went out to face the monster and answered correctly: "Man, in his infancy, his full growth, and when he totters on his staff in old age." The Sphinx gave a hoarse cry, and as it fled away Oedipus drove it over a precipice. The story seems to mean that a conundrum insoluble by the intellect was triumphantly solved in terms of common experience and life.

There is no adequate answer to that modern riddle of the Sphinx, the problem of evil, in purely intellectual terms. There is no neat reasoning whereby the heavy and the weary weight of all this unintelligible world may be lifted and taken away. Rachel weeping for her children, Job cursing his day, Socrates drinking the hemlock, St. Paul dying daily, St. Joan crying "My voices have deceived me"—Christianity itself has no formula explaining these things. Intellectually considered, the mystery remains a mystery. Neither theism

nor atheism, neither the philosophies nor the sciences
can solve this, the deepest problem for humanity. We do
not understand why this child is blind; nor why that
mother, for whom life has already been one long discipline, now loses her only son. If she herself understands
(and she probably does) it is because the true and
sufficient answer comes only out of life itself, life with
Christ's cross towering in triumph over it. The real issue
of life can be solved only in terms of life's experience,
and not of any intellectual theory. It is when the problem
of evil is deliberately shifted from the purely intellectual
to the practical plane—out of philosophers' classrooms
into the street, the hospital ward or the sanctuary—
that it becomes its own answer. The very belief in God
which creates and constitutes the intellectual riddle is
turned to truth by the test of life. That is Newbolt's
testimony in his lines on Clifton chapel:

> "This is the chapel; here, my son,
>   Your father thought the thoughts of youth,
>   And heard the words that one by one
>   The touch of life has turned to truth."

We owe the existence of our problem to the great
words of religion, and therefore it is to religion alone—
to faith authenticated in life and vindicated in experience
—that we have to turn, if our problem is to be triumphantly dealt with. Belief in God creates our problem; it
will be dealt with, therefore, by God or not at all. The
Author of our faith must be its Finisher; the Creator
must be the Redeemer; Deep calls to Deep, and that
Deep must give the answer.

> "My faith burns low, my hope burns low,
>   Only my heart's desire cries out in me;

By the deep thunder of its want and woe
Cries out, to Thee."

That is Christina Rossetti who, knowing that there is
"none other Lamb, none other Name," calls out of the
deep in faith.

"Where reason fails with all her powers,
There faith prevails and love adores."

That is Isaac Watts, and it is an almost perfect statement of that relation between reason and faith which
every man has to discover for himself.

Faith? Yes, most certainly. Faith is not blind credulity.
That we all live by faith of some sort is part of what it
means to be human. Not only have we a right to believe;
the necessity of belief is laid upon us. There can be no
question of the legitimacy of faith and its place in human
life as the presupposition of all knowledge. Progress in
scientific knowledge depends on it as much as does
progress in other kinds of knowledge made by poet or
saint.

Very well, if I am to give the Christian answer to our
problem—the answer, I mean, by which the Christian
really lives—you must allow me to be downright about
it. You would not thank me for any vague ambiguities.
As a Christian, I cannot make sense of this universe in
any way other than by faith in God, through Jesus
Christ—Incarnate, Crucified, Risen—and I submit that
it is faith at this, its highest level, which transforms our
problem of evil. Indeed, "transformation" is the key-
word which alone can unlock the door confronting us.
The existence of God as All-Great and All-Loving is
only fully credible if the evil in His world, in all its

reality, range and depth, is being conquered and transformed into good. Where the pessimistic voluptuary of the East confesses, ''There was a door to which I found no key'' and takes to cynicism and drink, the Christian triumphs in the transforming revelation of the Cross. It is out of life, with the Resurrection at the very centre of it, that the answer to the problem of evil is given. We turn, then, to the victory of the Cross.

Look at it first as a fact, an event in history. Here is a crime if there ever was one; no more flagrant example of injustice can be adduced than this; and if divine providence seems flatly contradicted anywhere in human history, it is here. At the Cross the whole human problem of suffering and sin comes to a burning focus. For here is the supreme instance of the problem we have been discussing all along. The Cross shows forth as does nothing else in history, the heinous actuality of sin, the nature of evil and its consequences. Indeed, what was suffered there is known for ever as The Passion. Look at the Cross; the world is such that in it this can happen; Calvary is the fate of the Prince of human life in a world like ours. There, where goodness was most unmixed and suffering most undeserved, the victory of evil was most signal and complete. We touch the nadir of moral evil in the crime which killed this Man of Sorrows. A world of men capable of compassing His death is capable of anything, any lesser wrong.

For it was Christ that died, no less. If history is the workshop of divine revelation; if the very mind and act of God are made known anywhere in terms of human life, they are made known in this human life. God has spoken to man in His Son; the Man called Christ is the Word, God's presence and His very self in time. Yet He, the Incarnate Word, was nailed to a gallows to die like a criminal.

But if you are going to look at the Cross as a fact, this is not all. This is not the whole of the concrete event by any means. For Jesus is more and other than the greatest of the martyrs. His Cross is far more than the supreme illustration of Lowell's lines about "truth for ever on the scaffold." He is not merely a passive victim in this drama, but an actor, and a Victor throughout, consciously and deliberately advancing to His death, laying down His life even when it is being taken from Him. "No man taketh my life from me; I lay it down of myself." His acquaintance with grief is deliberate. He steadfastly sets His face to go to Jerusalem; He is the conscious master of the situation, even in Gethsemane; standing before Pilate He is silent, refusing to plead; instead of Pilate judging Him, it is He who judges Pilate; He drinks the cup of His sufferings and death not of desire but of set purpose, because it is the purpose of the eternal God from the foundation of the world. Why? Well, if we will let His words and works speak, they proclaim that He came as God's representative, God's last word to men, to be identified with men wholly and to share with them all that humanity is and implies. And because in all things He is made like unto His brethren, tempted in all points like as they are, bearing their griefs and carrying their sorrows, even baptised with the baptism of sinners in Jordan, He travels that road to the uttermost. He is so completely identified with sinners that He shares all that sin means and involves. In this world of pain and sin He, who knew no sin, was "made sin" on our behalf. That hard saying of the Apostle seems to mean that the death on the Cross which he deliberately embraced is the baptism He had to be baptised with, and by which He was straitened until it should be accomplished, and He would say "It is finished." That alone could fully disclose what evil is and means in God's universe. Its wage is death, and He alone fully knows it and says Amen to it on behalf of humanity. Therefore, He goes to death with His eyes open; He refuses the anæsthetic; "when He had tasted thereof He would not drink." It was in all the majesty of a love which was utterly clear-sighted and never sentimental, which had not a trace of self-pity but went out in holiness to sinners to the end, that He endured the Cross and despised the shame.

Yet here is the paradox; this death which completes His entire identification with men, isolates Him from them utterly. It is the loneliest death in all history. Pilate washes his hands of Him; the soldiers dress Him up and spit at Him; the crowd roars and jeers; the priests gloat in triumph; all the venom of the human heart is concentrated in the taunt, "If Thou be the Son of God, come down from the Cross"; even the thieves hanging there with Him cast the same in His teeth; and as for His intimate friends, they are not there; they have either betrayed Him or denied Him or fled. He was forsaken. The Abbé Loisy was once speaking to a friend about that passage in St. John's gospel which gives us the familiar picture of the two figures at the foot of the Cross, the mother of Jesus and the disciple, and he said "No, this was a development of the original story; it is magnificent, but it isn't history." Whether the Abbé was right or not, his insight was right. Christ died in utter loneliness and at the last He cried, "My God, My God, why hast Thou forsaken me?" None of the hundreds of commentaries, ancient or modern, on that Cry of Dereliction can tell you just what it means; no one can know. He who alone knew how grievous sin is to God was staggering there under the whole weight of it; which is not the least part of the meaning in those tremendous words, ''He descended into Hell.''

There, then, is the fact of the Cross, and though the Christian knows it as a triumphant fact—though he can never look at it in isolation from the Resurrection with which it is indissolubly united—it is, nevertheless, a scandalous and offensive fact; and the vital point is that the Christian religion, so far from shrinking from it, has ever pointed to it and insisted on it. Indeed, by facing evil, and facing it here, and by not belittling or ignoring it, Christianity has greatly deepened and intensified the age-long problem which evil raises. We haven't seen the problem of sorrow and sin in all their inescapable horror until we have stood at the Cross. The Church has never ceased to insist that the Cross—to the Jews a stumbling block and to the Greeks foolishness—is ''crucial'' for its faith. That is, it has always refused to explain suffering and sin away; it has looked physical evil and moral evil in the face, as nothing else has done. The rivals of the Christian faith fail just where the message of the Cross is proclaimed.

Look, for example, at Epicureanism and Stoicism, those philosophies of antiquity which live on under other names. Each virtually proposes to make us invulnerable in some way; each tries to provide armour that is impenetrable to the slings and arrows of outrageous fortune. They offer back-doors of escape from pain and woe; the one by defiant resistance—''Eat, drink and be merry, for to-morrow you die''; the other by a cold inhuman detachment, or by suicide after the high Roman fashion.[1] We are to be made immune; from sin, by the recognition that it is a vulgar prejudice; and from suffering, by sternly living it down as a discreditable fancy. But Christianity has always refused to admit that the alleged immunity is real or possible. It denies that these inoculations work. Taking its stand at the Cross, it makes twofold answer.

First, about suffering. It knows that suffering is a terrible reality. To quote some words of Baron von Hügel, "It pointed to Jesus with the terror of Death upon Him in Gethsemane, with a cry of desolation upon the Cross of Calvary; it allowed the soul, it encouraged the soul, to sob itself out." Surely He hath borne our griefs and carried our sorrows; in all our afflictions He is afflicted. The pains He had to bear may not give you and me a theory about pain, but they help us to bear pain. Men and women have not been mistaken in their conviction that He who triumphed through pain is with them in all their darkness and suffering.

Second, about sin. Christianity knows that sin, too, is a terrible reality. The Cross is a mirror in which we see our own sin as we had never seen it before. Evils which we had either minimised or ignored are reflected here with piercing clearness. We suddenly realise that the sins of the Pharisees, of Pilate, of the High Priest, are not unique; which of us is sure that he would not have done the same, or that he himself does not crucify Christ anew? "All men may have forsaken Him," we think to ourselves, "yet would we have not; we would not

---

[1] For the substance and phrasing of this and the preceding sentence I am largely indebted to a paragraph by Dr. Inge, which I cannot now trace.

have been found consenting unto His death; we would not have slain the Holy One and the Just." But can we be so sure? Could Clovis, king of the barbarian Franks, be sure, for example, when—on being converted to Christianity and hearing for the first time the story of the Cross—he burst out, "Had I been there with my victorious Franks, I would have avenged His injuries." His very confidence, and the way in which he expresses it, make us wonder how much this crafty and ambitious savage had seen of the real meaning of the Cross. But is the assumption true for Clovis or for any man? Can we consider ourselves and our world for one moment, can we read any modern newspaper for two minutes, and be so sure? The truth is that no man can dissociate himself from the scandal of the Cross. Though sturdy common sense says that he may certainly plead an alibi, those simple songs of black people in America come nearer to the truth. The "Negro Spirituals," as they are called, show a spiritual rather than a matter-of-fact insight into the story of the Cross, and it is a truer insight. There is one song which asks relentlessly, "When they crucified my Lord, were you there?" Yes, we were there; we *are* there; the whole race is there; there the first Adam and the second, the natural man and the Man from Heaven, are come together. I only know what my sin is when I face the fact of the Cross.

But we cannot stop there, for the Cross is more than a fact. an historical event. Look at it in the second place as the transforming revelation which Christians have always found it to be. Through this concrete event in time there is an eternal note beating. God was acting there in such a triumphant way that an officer of the Roman army standing by on duty was moved to cry,

"Truly this man was the Son of God." He saw, however dimly, what men have not failed to see ever since, that here something was breaking into history from beyond history. God was in Christ making a supreme self-disclosure, and the Cross of Christ was the deepest visible expression of it; the Word from the Beyond for our human predicament here reaches the climax of its utterance.

I quoted the confident boast of King Clovis just now, "Had I been there, etc." Let me put another quotation beside it from Richard Jefferies' book *Bevis*. In that classic about boyhood you find this: "The crucifixion hurt his feelings very much: the cruel nails, the unfeeling spear: he looked at the picture a long time, and then turned over the page saying, 'If God had been there He would not have let them do it.' " If God had been there! For a Christian, dramatic irony can go no further, since the whole of the Christian religion rests on the fact that God *was* there; the Cross is the mightiest of the mighty acts of God. Out of this supreme manifestation of evil and in terms of its very stuff, has come the sublimest and most triumphant manifestation of good. What is intrinsically and in isolation a terrible crime, has come to be the occasion of the world's greatest blessing. For it is a matter of experience that out of the lowest depth to which the race could go down, God made His highest revelation; out of man's uttermost God's uttermost was fashioned; I cannot get away, here, from the old language in all its majesty and comfort, "just there where sin did abound, grace did the more abound"; that is, God's mind and act of love are shown forth out of the very stuff of events which supremely illustrate man's mind and act. It is as though a cosmic battle were being fought out on that neutral timber of the Cross between the sin of Man and the redeeming love of God. The Cross is the arena for the fight between the Powers of Evil and Christ the Power of God. This metaphor of conflict between Evil and God's grace—of Holy Love which fights and conquers by suffering to the uttermost—is one of the oldest metaphors in Christian theology; the New Testament is full of it. Sin ''sets the pace'' as it were; in its contest against redeeming Love Sin chooses the ground where the battle is to be fought out; ''This is the Heir, come let us kill *Him*.'' Sin chooses the weapons. Sin sets up a gallows and God sets His love upon the gallows commending His love towards us at so great a cost. The only language that will do here is that language of amazement and gratitude which fills the New Testament. While we were yet sinners Christ died for us; He endured the contradiction of sinners against Himself; when He was reviled He reviled not again, when He suffered He threatened not. And herein we know the love of God toward us; we know it as a conquering love which broke the bands of death for us and therefore breaks our stony hearts as nothing else can. At the Cross we see God using our sin as the instrument of our redemption; His best is given in terms of our worst. God was there, reconciling us to Himself.

When I was at school in Surrey we used to go sometimes to a large natural amphitheatre in the sparsely-wooded chalk hills. The white road entered it and ran straight up over the great concavity of grass and thorn-bushes until it climbed into the sky at the top and there vanished from sight. And on that hard horizon-line of the ridge there stood a tree, a beech which seemed to have disengaged itself from the other trees, and to stand solitary. We called the place "the end of the world"; as we went up the steep road to that tree, it seemed like coming to the very edge of all things and preparing to look over into the abyss. Well, the ultimate fact in human history is a Tree; beyond it there is and can be nothing. God Himself can do nothing more; greater love is impossible; the uttermost even of the infinite grace of God is there. The Cross is not only a scandalous fact of history; it is the triumphant act of God. It is not only man's deed of sin but God's deed of grace. It is the Lord's doing and it is marvellous in our eyes. [1]

But this transforming revelation is misrepresented and robbed of its meaning if it is separated from the victory of the Resurrection, with which it forms an indissoluble unity. The Resurrection is not a new event tacked on to the foregoing; it is Calvary seen in all its triumphant meaning as the act of God. The Cross is "marvellous" not only because of its moral power over my stubborn heart, but, more fundamentally, because it defeats man's enemy, Evil, and therefore his last enemy—the physical evil called Death. That was the glowing conviction which made and makes the Church. All the evidence of the New Testament goes to show that the burden of the good news or gospel was not "Follow this teacher and do your best," but "Jesus and the Resurrection." You cannot take that away from Christianity without radically altering its character and destroying its identity. It is the

---

[1] Perhaps I have hardly made it sufficiently clear that there was *actual* transformation of evil to good on the Cross. The words "Father, forgive them" are historic fact. We do not always realise that the love of God is just as much an historic reality in the Crucifixion, as the suffering through sin. "Christus Victor" is no mere rhetoric; His victory was a new and constitutive event in history.

presupposition, explicit or implicit, of every sentence in
the New Testament. In the Cross Christianity sees not
merely a striking illustration of the Sublime, but the
Sublime in omnipotent action. ''Behold and see if there
be any sorrow like unto His sorrow. Is it nothing to you,
all ye that pass by?'' The answer is that it would be
nothing to us—no more, at any rate, than the suffering
of many another nameless and unremembered martyr—
if the Passion had ended with the Cry of Dereliction in
the darkness, if it had ''come to nothing.'' If our
problem is only intensified by the Cross; if He came, not
to the rescue like a second Adam, but only to the old
hopeless fight against sin and death with its old foregone
conclusion, why should mortals single Him out, this
fellow-mortal, for commiseration? If He is only one
more unfortunate gone to His death—well, that's that.
We, too, have to die.

The fact is that the Jesus who merely illustrates general
religious sentiments is neither the Jesus of the New
Testament nor the living Lord of the Church of the
Apostles and Martyrs. Without the conviction which
possessed Christian men from the beginning and which
was and is the very basis and *raison d'être* of the Church—
that Jesus Christ overcame sin and death and is alive for
ever; that He was really victorious in this strife and could
not be held by the grave—without that fact of the
Resurrection I do not see that there is uniqueness in
Christ, nor any real redemption and victory. Unless we
are to be muddled by mere rhetoric here we have to
choose between a Jesus with whom ''the President of
the Immortals had finished His sport'' and the Christ
who is the Power of God, going down like a celestial
Samson into Hades, carrying away the gates, leading

captivity captive and bringing life and immortality to light. You have to choose between complete irrationality at the very heart of things and this triumph of the love which moves the stars.

Since it is my business to try to state what the specifically Christian answer to the problem of evil is, let me repeat that belief in the Resurrection is not an appendage to the Christian faith; it *is* the Christian faith; it is its only sufficient basis and guarantee. It is not tacked on at the end of the story to make a happy ending; it is implicit in the story from the beginning; it *is* from the foundation of the world. We can't begin to comprehend how it happened; the gospels cannot explain the Resurrection; it is the Resurrection which alone explains the gospels. The Resurrection is a mighty act of God, strange to all experience, inscrutable to all science, repudiated and sometimes ridiculed by much that is considered the best intellect and finest culture of our day; but to those who believe the astounding fact and bring it to the test of life, sharing in the fellowship not only of Christ's sufferings but also of His Triumph—here is the real solution to the problem of evil. It is real because it springs out of life and has been tested and vindicated there by uncounted generations of faithful men. Moreover, Christians are not sentimentalists, living in a world of phantasy where the wish is father to the thought. We know well enough that we still sin, suffer and die; the fragmentariness and pain of life are not taken away; we do not yet see these things put under our feet. But we see Jesus crowned, with a victory in which we already share and which Death itself cannot touch. We know Him as the Captain of our salvation, the living Lord of human life. Are we, then, merely the pathetic victims of credulity? Is this Faith just so much ''dope''?

I am not prepared to deny that much which has been said and done in the name of religion is ''dope,'' and worse; all that I am asserting is that to dismiss this testimony of the Christian centuries is as easy as it is unconvincing. The highest that I know comes to me with compelling authority in the Cross. I cannot escape it. There the Eternal God speaks His ''last word'' to me, and I merely add my testimony to that of an uncounted multitude when I say that there is the peace and comfort that I want, the forgiveness and power that I need.

CHAPTER IV

Listeners' Questions

T O receive from strangers over five hundred letters in a fortnight—some of them long, many of them able and searching, and almost all of them charmingly courteous—is a very tantalising privilege, especially for one who believes in the duty of answering letters. I feel like a man who has accidentally locked himself out of his house just after he has turned the bathroom tap full on. To answer these essays (for that is what most of them are), is a physical impossibility. After reading them all through once, I wished that I were Prospero with Ariel to do my bidding, and that he could fly to each of my correspondents in turn, carrying the bagful of letters sent by all the others. Believe me, you would all learn a lot, as I have done.

For the dominant impression left on my mind by a great number of these letters is that they cancel one another out. At least, they answer one another even if they fail to answer the riddle. Indeed, they remind me of Sidney Smith's remark after witnessing a noisy argument between two women who were standing at their doors and facing one another across the street. As he turned away he said to his friend, ''These women will never agree because they argue from different premis(s)es.'' Exactly! These stimulating letters leave the reader a little depressed because they do just that. Let me offer com-

ments on a large number of letters, then, by giving you
typical examples of these different premisses from which
people start.

First of all, not a few earnest people would solve and
dismiss the immemorial problem of evil by quoting
texts from Holy Scripture. They argue like this: ''Why
waste time with human theories when there is a divine
answer in the Bible? See Deuteronomy chapter so-and-so,
verse so-and-so.'' Well, when Ariel arrived with the
bag, if these correspondents would devote twelve solid
hours to reading its contents, they would realise that
intelligent people whose faith is surely as real and fruitful
as their own, cannot read the Bible ''in the flat'' like
that. Any man, for example, who reads the Old Testament with understanding will discover that there are at
least *five* distinct and different answers to the problem of
suffering in that corpus of writings; they spring from
different periods of history and belong to different
levels of spiritual vision. The modern man is not im-
pressed, therefore, by the mere citation of texts; he
rightly wants to understand them, in their context. His
very certainty that the Scriptures are the fount of divine
wisdom—that it is indeed the Word of God which is
spoken to him in the words of the Bible—has set him
free from the bondage of the letter, the prison-house of
verbal infallibility.

It is no use shilly-shallying here; loyalty to truth in the
shape of literary and historical criticism forbids it. A
Christian knows that he has to serve God with the mind
as well as with heart and will, and that the obligation to
be intelligent is itself a moral obligation. The Bible is
abused when it is used merely as an armoury of proof-
texts for defending some theological scheme (a game at

which more than one can play, notoriously enough). We use the Bible rightly only when, to quote Luther, we see that it is the cradle wherein Christ is laid; that is, when we worship the Holy Child and not His crib. These letters have renewed my conviction that blind bibliolatry can be as pathetically wrong as what is called blind unbelief, and that the way of obscurantism is the way to disaster.

A second batch of letters starts from entirely different premisses. These would solve the riddle of the origin of human suffering and of the diversity of human conditions by a confident appeal, not to the Bible nor to anything in human experience, but to something lying entirely beyond experience. They begin with the hypothesis, which can be neither proved nor disproved, of Karma or Reincarnation. That is, they adopt the classic assumption of Hindu thought that human souls have been transmigrating through a successive series of reincarnations from the beginning, and that your lot and mine in this world is only the result in strict justice of what we were and what we did in former existences. One of my correspondents delights in the ''superb justice'' of this theory, and several upbraid the Christian Church for ignoring it instead of believing and proclaiming it. To this challenge I would make a threefold reply.

First, this doctrine of Reincarnation virtually abandons the problem of evil by throwing it into the unknown. It rests on sheer conjecture, lifting the root of the problem out of human life and transplanting it into a cosmic past which is safe from all mortal scrutiny. To solve our problem by referring it to the unknown and the unknowable, is to confess that thought is bankrupt. Just as no traveller returns from that undiscovered country beyond death, so no one can return to the undiscoverable country beyond birth. To account for the present as a debt contracted in a former existence is surely as objectionable as banking on the hereafter. That, of course, is what Christians have often done, but I suppose and hope that most of us would agree in condemning it. I refer to the crude notion that you can account satisfactorily for the woe of the world and the cruel unfairness of many a man's lot by saying that the balance will be amply redressed in Heaven. This is especially objectionable when it is made an excuse for neglecting social duty here and now. The quietism which virtually says that we need not bother about the new social order which we need so desperately, because "there is a pie in the sky when you die," is a blasphemous caricature of the gospel. Well, the doctrine of Reincarnation does something very like this only it does it backwards. Its fatalism is just as bad as Christian Quietism.

The second objection is that my alleged pre-existence can have no present moral meaning simply because I am debarred from remembering anything about it. The sense of responsibility is always bound up with memory; eliminate that, and punishment has no moral worth and therefore no moral justification.

In the third place this doctrine of Reincarnation knows nothing of what the Christian means by Redemption. It is sheer legalism. It proclaims that the scheme of things is a ruthlessly mechanical and impersonal system of action and award, whereas the Gospel proclaims that God is love, coming to meet us in our felt insufficiency with all the majesty and comfort of His grace. The conception of God's redeeming grace—that is, His love in action—is the last word of the Old Testament and the

key-word of the New. If St. Paul's epistles do not mean
that God's way of redemption is altogether higher than
the way of superb justice, they do not mean anything.
Indeed, there is not a shred of evidence for this doctrine
of Karma or a series of Reincarnations in the New
Testament; it is incompatible with the very genius of
Christianity and is therefore no part of the Christian
answer to the problem of evil.

There is a third and fairly considerable pile of letters
which start from still other premisses; they argue that
we have the testimony not only of Scripture in general,
but of Christ Himself, that the sin and woe of the world
are due to the Devil or Satan. Perhaps I may refer my
correspondents to what I said about this important
question in the third section of my first talk, adding here
that I am in large agreement with them if I may be
allowed to state the argument in my own way and to
utter two caveats about it.

First of all, I agree that though it is now common to
joke about the Devil we have to take the question
seriously, as more than one distinguished modern
thinker does. You may remember a picture in *Punch*
some years ago which showed two little girls playing
together, when one asked the other, ''Do you believe
in the Devil?'' The reply was, ''Of course not, silly; it's
like Santa Claus, it's only Daddy.'' We jest like that
because we very properly disavow all crude nonsense
about a Devil with two horns and a tail, and because
Christian people cannot believe in anything which
implies an anti-God, a positive principle of evil equally
self-subsistent with God, uncreated by Him and eternally
hostile. To erect a metaphysic of that kind of Christ's
language about Satan is, as I argued in my first talk,

quite indefensible. Indeed, most of us will appreciate the reply of the notorious John Wilkes to a heckler at the hustings in the eighteenth century. When the man shouted from the crowd "I'd rather vote for the Devil than for you," Wilkes replied, "What if your friend won't stand?"

Some of you ask me, therefore, whether I think that Jesus, in speaking of "this daughter of Abraham whom Satan hath bound," was merely using the thought-forms of His day which have since been abandoned. My answer is Yes and No. First, it is clear that if the Incarnation is not to be emptied of all real meaning, Jesus was fully and completely man, living under the conditions of empirical humanity in Palestine in the first century. He did use the categories of His age, speaking as does the rest of the New Testament about the Evil One, Satan, the Enemy. We could not expect Him to do anything else without surrendering our conviction of His true Manhood.

But on the other hand, Jesus was surely uttering a profound and inescapable truth when He used those vivid and dramatic thought-forms of His day about the Power of Darkness. It is more than legitimate for us to argue that there is a gigantic Power of Evil in the universe; we can't avoid doing so. We believe that Good is more than terrestrial—more, that is, than a domestic affair peculiar to this wayside planet. It is cosmic; like the other great values it is, we believe, eternal in the heavens; it has a continued extra-mundane existence. Very well; we see terrible evil in this world also; it is a roaring lion going its devouring way among us; there is often a fearful intensification or speeding up of evil in human experience which needs some explanation; we see men living and dying under its tyranny. If we believe, then, in the continued extra-mundane existence of good, there is already some ground for believing in the continued extra-mundane existence of evil; and it is to this that Jesus Christ undoubtedly bears witness. He does so in vivid oriental imagery, speaking of conflict and victory. As I said in my first talk, in doing so He is not constructing a philosophical solution to the problem of evil but pointing to an obvious fact of religious experience and to a task for the will of man. And His victory is a cosmic victory; though there is evil in God's universe, it is to be overcome by God. Christ is the Victor in the strife.

Now for my two caveats. First of all, it is dangerous to justify language about the Devil as a usefully vivid and personalised way of describing these grim facts of life. We have to beware of thinking of Satan as a second God, as though the cosmic issue were in any doubt. That which is a liar from the beginning will have an end. Evil does carry within itself the seeds of its own destruction. God reigns. In the second place, we have to beware of letting this argument for the reality and limited activity of extra-mundane evil in any way lessen our own sense of moral responsibility. We have to beware of blaming the Devil and thereby making an excuse for man's sin. Jesus Christ never did this; to lose our inalienable sense of moral accountability in this way would be to lose our humanity. What the Bible calls the Devil is one of the conditions of our environment as we know it; the important and vital truth is that we are more than conquerors through Him who loved us.

So much then for scores of letters which argue from one or other of these different premisses. You will notice, moreover, that they all agree in this—that Evil

is a reality; whether an infallible Book, or the Law of
Karma or the Devil be their starting point, all recognise
the reality of Evil in God's universe.

I pass now to a fourth batch of some thirty or forty
letters which start from the opposite presupposition.
They argue not from life's grim experience but from a
philosophical theory which explains that experience
away by denying that evil is real. Evil exists only in
semblance; it is the negation or privation of good. It is
not the presence of anything but the absence of something, just as darkness is merely the absence of light (an
illustration which several people have used). In short,
evil has no positive existence and therefore God who is
the cause of all that exists is not the cause of it. It *lacks* a
cause. God is therefore absolved of responsibility for the
evil in His universe since, properly considered, evil is not
"really" evil. Admittedly, these absences or deprivations
of good are depressing; they do hinder the full realisation
of the Good. Why then (if this is all that Evil really is)
are they allowed to occur? The answer given by monism
or pantheism in its many forms, and notably by two
great thinkers of antiquity, Plotinus and S. Augustine,
is that this apparent evil is an ingredient or condition of
good: what does seem evil in isolation is ultimately good
when related to all else, as part of a great whole. S.
Augustine and his friends once watched two cocks
fighting and decided that the miserable and dejected look
of the defeated bird somehow added to the splendid
exhibition of energy in the fight, and heightened their
own interest in it.[1] And many of my correspondents put

---

[1] Augustine, *De Ordine* ii. 4, quoted by P. H. Wicksteed; *Reactions between Dogma and Philosophy*, pp. 246, 318.

the word evil in inverted commas in a similar way, and for a similar reason.

In addition to what I have already tried to say about this theory in the second section of my first talk, let me suggest the following considerations. First of all, there are dozens of letters in Ariel's bag—heart-rending stories of bereavement, suffering and sin "here where men sit and hear each other groan"—which make this optimistic monism look little better than sophistry. There are letters here which make S. Augustine's contention that only what endures immutably can be said to exist, palpably untrue to experience. The few people who have pooh-poohed the faith-healer of Deal have not really dealt with him. Nor do they face the fearful problem of downright human wickedness, like cruelty to children or animals, or like the recent triumph of barbarism over bravery in Abyssinia. S. Augustine's argument that though sin has its seat in an evil will yet that evil will is only a defect of good will, is surely word-play at best. He knew the reality and power of sin if anyone ever did, but he argues that the evil will is the result of our not setting the will on God. But surely this means that we set it on something else; it is positive volition just the same.

After all, we do find evil in the world of our experience and therefore we are confronted with the dilemma which none of the letters in this batch seem to have noticed. It is this. If this universe *appears* to us not to be perfect, can it be so in reality? Is not its failure to seem perfect itself an imperfection? For, if we are right, the universe is, admittedly, not rational. If we are wrong, *we* are not rational. But we are part of the universe. Therefore the very fact that the universe can produce creatures to whom it seems imperfect, is itself a problem.

I suggest to you that evil is objectively real; life is too eloquent of sin and pain for theory to discredit its reality; we have to fight these things and extract good out of them rather than explain them away. Thomas Aquinas is surely right in saying that evil is evil until a man rises to that width of vision which reveals the transcendent power of God transforming evil into good. The Cross is the supreme instance of the fact that the worst evil faced in the right way can be made to yield some good not attainable in any other way: we can believe that all the time we are fighting against evil and trying to destroy it utterly we are forcing it to contribute to the ultimate good. Evil is real, and we cannot run away from the fact. Some of my correspondents, seeing this, admit the reality of evil but argue that just as light implies its opposite darkness, and virtue logically involves vice, so good could not exist without evil. To this I would reply that virtue involves not vice, but potential vice: it is the possibility of evil, not the existence of evil, which is necessary to the highest good. I mean that it is only in a world where wickedness *can* happen, that gentleness, heroism and love *will* happen. It is the possibility of evil in God's world which is the necessary means to that highest good which we call the Kingdom of God. For God is Love.

This at once leads to several very interesting letters which start from the premiss of God's omnipotence. That is, they tackle the dilemma which makes the problem of evil the age-long enigma that it is. The familiar argument goes as follows: Granted that the greatest ultimate good is the perfection of man's moral personality; if God is all powerful He could surely have devised a way of achieving this without the suffering and evil which we know. To argue that He could not, is at once to limit His power. If God is omnipotent love how can the possibility of evil be inevitable?

Well, I have said all along that I do not believe there is any adequate solution to this logical dilemma in purely intellectual terms. I believe that it is life not logic, which speaks the language of truth here. The Christian finds his theory of knowledge in the Incarnation. With that qualification, then, let me now add something to what I said in the first two talks.

First of all, what do you mean by Omnipotence? Does it mean power to determine arbitrarily what shall be possible? Almost all philosophers answer No. God cannot do what is in itself absurd; make a false statement true for example; make virtue vice or a circle square; He cannot cause anything to exist and not-to-exist at the same time; He cannot destroy Himself.[1] These propositions are intrinsically absurd because they are meaningless. You remember the old conundrum: What would happen if an irresistible force met an immovable body? The answer is, of course, that the question doesn't mean anything. So here. Questions fatal to the omnipotence they presuppose are clearly meaningless. Omnipotence cannot mean the capacity to effect a contradiction; it can only mean power to do what is consistent with God's nature and perfection.

God is the Ground of all that is. There are eternal verities (the truths of mathematics or of logic, for example), and the sum of them is the mode in which God exists and acts. What is possible depends on what is actual; that is, it depends on what God is. These eternal

[1] See A. E. Taylor, article on "Theism," *Encyclopaedia of Religion and Ethics*, xii, 261 b.

truths are not prior to God, as though they were independent laws to which He has to conform. Nor are they subsequent to God and the product of His will, as though He were a being for whom Truth was not valid until He had decided what should constitute Truth. ''I am that I am'' is the truth about God and His universe. And because God is essentially self-consistent the word omnipotence cannot be used to maintain a contrary proposition.

In the second place, then, God has a character. He is known for what He is by what He does in history. He is not an indeterminate Absolute transcending all distinctions, a mystic Whole for whom possibilities and impossibilities are alike. If I may quote what I have learned from a distinguished philosopher, Dr. Tennant, of Cambridge—to exist is to be this and not that, even for God. He is a determinate being. For example, if He is love, He cannot be hate. In that He wills an evolutionary order He does not will a statically perfect paradise.

In the third place, then, His sovereignty is the sovereignty not of arbitrariness, but of love. The moral progress which my correspondents admit to be the ultimate good is surely a value which is only realisable in a finite world of freedom and development, not in a paradise of static perfection from the very beginning. If there is to be a developing moral order, the possibility of moral evil seems inevitable: it is the risk—humanly speaking—which God takes, though we cannot but believe that He triumphs over evil in the end.

God the Creator has made us free, free to be creators ourselves and to initiate good or evil, free to vindicate the moral order or to defy it. A creature who can defy

God is a far greater proof of God's omnipotence than a perfect Robot which could only act in blind obedience. It is the power to withhold his obedience which makes man's obedience worth while. Thomas Traherne puts this point forcibly and neatly when he says: "He seemeth to have made as many things depend upon man's liberty as His own. When all that could be wrought by the use of His own liberty was attained, by man's liberty He attained more." That is, the very proof of Love's omnipotence lies in its treatment of us, not as puppets, but as persons; not as slaves, but as sons. After all, the most remarkable thing about the Mastership of Jesus is that He never insists on being Master. He says that if you love Him you will keep His commandments; that is all there is to it. But it's everything.

BOOKS SUGGESTED FOR FURTHER READING.

1. GENERAL.

Studies in Theology. James Denney. Hodder & Stoughton, 1899. O.P.

The Philosophy of the Good Life. Charles Gore. Everyman Library, 1935. 4s.

**A Study of Religion.* James Martineau. O.P.

Foundations of Faith: I. Theological. W. E. Orchard. Allen & Unwin, 1924. O.P.

**The Idea of God.* A. S. Pringle-Pattison. Oxford University Press, 1920. 18s.

2. SPECIAL MONOGRAPHS, CHAPTERS OR ARTICLES.

Article on *Good and Evil* in the *Encyclopaedia of Religion and Ethics,* Vol. VI.

The Pain of this World and the Providence of God. M. C. D'Arcy, S.J. Longmans. O.P.

The Mystery of Pain. James Hinton. Allenson. O.P.

The fourth essay in *Essays and Addresses* (First Series). F. von Hügel. Dent, 1921. 8s. 6d.

**The Theory of Good and Evil.* H. Rashdall. Oxford University Press. 1907. 2 vols. 25s.

The Element of Pain and Conflict in Human Life. F. R. Tennant. Cambridge University Press. 4s. 6d.

God and the Struggle for Existence. Various Authors. Student Christian Movement Press. O.P.

Why do Men Suffer? Leslie Weatherhead. Student Christian Movement Press, 1935. 7s. 6d.

With the exception of those marked with an asterisk the books in this list are not too big and technical for the general reader.

O.P. means out of print. These books may be obtained secondhand or in libraries.

www.ingramcontent.com/pod-product-compliance
Lightning Source LLC
Chambersburg PA
CBHW030813090426
42737CB00010B/1262